To

_____

_____

From

_____

_____

_____

For my lovely sister, Dilly   S. W.

Written and compiled by Lois Rock
Illustrations copyright © 2012 Sophy Williams
This edition copyright © 2012 Lion Hudson

The moral rights of the author and illustrator
have been asserted

A Lion Children's Book
an imprint of
Lion Hudson plc
Wilkinson House, Jordan Hill Road,
Oxford OX2 8DR, England
www.lionhudson.com
ISBN 978 0 7459 6302 0

First edition 2012
1 3 5 7 9 10 8 6 4 2 0

Acknowledgments
Every effort has been made to trace and contact copyright owners for material used in this book. We apologize
for any inadvertent omissions or errors.

All unattributed prayers are by Lois Rock, copyright © Lion Hudson. Prayers by Jenni Dutton, Christina
Goodings, Sophie Piper, and Victoria Tebbs are copyright © Lion Hudson.

Bible extracts are taken or adapted from the Good News Bible published by the Bible Societies and
HarperCollins Publishers, © American Bible Society 1994, used with permission.

The Lord's Prayer (on page 22) from *Common Worship: Services and Prayers for the Church of England* (Church House
Publishing, 2000) is copyright © The English Language Liturgical Consultation, 1988 and is reproduced by
permission of the publishers.

The Poem-Book of the Gael: Translation from Irish Gaelic poetry into English prose and verse, selected and edited by
Eleanor Hull; London: Chatto & Windus, 1913.

Prayer by Blessed Teresa of Calcutta (on page 42) used by permission.

"We give thanks for domestic animals" (on page 55) by Michael Leunig is © Michael Leunig,
used by permission.

Carmina Gadelica collected by Alexander Carmichael is published by Floris Books, Edinburgh.

A catalogue record for this book is available
from the British Library

Typeset in 15/18 Lapidary 333 BT
Printed in China June 2012 (manufacturer LH17)

Distributed by:
UK: Marston Book Services Ltd, PO Box 269, Abingdon, Oxon OX14 4YN
USA: Trafalgar Square Publishing, 814 N Franklin Street, Chicago, IL 60610
USA Christian Market: Kregel Publications, PO Box 2607, Grand Rapids, MI 49501

The Lion Classic
Prayer Collection

Written and compiled by LOIS ROCK

Illustrated by SOPHY WILLIAMS

LION
CHILDREN'S

CONTENTS

CONTENTS

PRAYER

The prayer of speaking
the prayer of listening;
the prayer of kneeling
the prayer of walking;
the prayer of working
the prayer of playing;
the prayer of giving
the prayer of receiving;
the prayer of laughing
the prayer of weeping;
the prayer of loving
the prayer of forgiving;
the prayer of living
till life's ending.

GOD IS NEAR

Who shall enter the house of the Lord?
Who shall stand in his holy place?

The one whose hands are clean of wrongdoing.
The one whose thoughts are good and pure.

BASED ON PSALM 24

In the rush and noise of life, as you have intervals, step within
yourselves and be still. Wait upon God and feel his good presence;
this will carry you through your day's business.

WILLIAM PENN (1644–1718)

O make my heart so still, so still,
When I am deep in prayer,
That I might hear the white mist-wreaths
Losing themselves in air!

Prayer from Japan

God help my thoughts! They stray from me, setting off on the wildest journeys; when I am at prayer, they run off like naughty children, making trouble. When I read the Bible, they fly to a distant place, filled with seductions. My thoughts can cross an ocean with a single leap; they can fly from earth to heaven, and back again, in a single second. They come to me for a fleeting moment, and then away they flee. No chains, no locks can hold them back; no threats of punishment can restrain them, no hiss of a lash can frighten them. They slip from my grasp like tails of eels, they swoop hither and thither like swallows in flight.

Dear Christ, who can see into every heart, and read every mind, take hold of my thoughts. Bring my thoughts back to me, and clasp me to yourself.

Author unknown

Thinking of heaven

A low prayer, a high prayer, I send through space.
Arrange them Thyself, O thou King of Grace.

From The Poem-Book of the Gael

Come into my soul, Lord,
as the dawn breaks into the sky;
let your sun rise in my heart
at the coming of the day.

Traditional

Looking at the sky
while a tall tree sways,
I hear God speaking
in a thousand different ways:
of melodies and miracles
that all are born on earth;
of dreams and possibilities
of everlasting worth.

Sophie Piper

PRAYING WITH THE BIBLE

Jesus said:
Ask, and you will receive;
seek, and you will find;
knock, and the door will be opened to you.

For everyone who asks will receive,
and anyone who seeks will find,
and the door will be opened to those who knock.

Your Father in heaven will give good things to
those who ask him.

FROM MATTHEW 7:7–8, 11

PRAISING GOD

Praise the Lord from heaven,
all beings of the height!
Praise him, holy angels
and golden sun so bright.

Praise him, silver moonlight,
praise him, every star!
Let your praises shine
throughout the universe so far.

Praise the Lord from earth below,
all beings of the deep!
Lightning flash! You thunder, roar!
You ocean creatures, leap.

Praise him, hill and mountain!
Praise him, seed and tree.
Praise him, all you creatures
that run the wide world free.

Let the mighty praise him.
Let the children sing.
Men and women, young and old:
Praise your God and king.

FROM PSALM 148

The sunrise
tells of God's glory;
the moonrise
tells of God's glory;
the starshine
tells of God's glory;
the heavens
tell of God's glory.

BASED ON PSALM 19

I praise the Lord with all my soul,
my strength, my heart, my mind:
he blesses me with love and grace
and is for ever kind.

BASED ON PSALM 103:1–4

Praise the Lord with trumpets
all praise to him belongs;
praise him with your music
your dancing and your songs!

BASED ON PSALM 150

Obeying God

O Lord,
I have heard your laws.
May I worship you.
May I worship you alone.
May all I say and do show respect for your holy name.
May I honour the weekly day of rest.
May I show respect for my parents.
May I reject violence so that I never take a life.
May I learn to be loyal in friendship and so learn to be faithful
in marriage.
May I not steal what belongs to others.
May I not tell lies to destroy another person's reputation.
May I not be envious of what others have, but may I learn to be
content with the good things you give me.

BASED ON THE TEN COMMANDMENTS, EXODUS 20

O Lord,
Keep me from wrongdoing;
for the wicked are nothing more than wisps of straw in the
autumn gale.
O Lord, help me obey your will;
for the righteous are like trees that grow by the life-giving river,
bearing leaves and fruit in their season.

BASED ON PSALM 1

Teach me, Lord, the meaning of your laws,
and I will obey them at all times.
Keep me obedient to your commandments,
because in them I find happiness.
Your word is a lamp to guide me
and a light for my path.

PSALM 119:33, 35, 105

Teach me, O God,
to do what is just,
to show constant love
and to live in fellowship with you.

BASED ON MICAH 6:8

Seeking forgiveness

Come back to the Lord your God.
He is kind and full of mercy;
he is patient and keeps his promise;
he is always ready to forgive and not punish.

JOEL 2:13

I told God everything:
I told God about all the wrong things I had done.
I gave up trying to pretend.
I gave up trying to hide.
I knew that the only thing to do was to confess.

And God forgave me.

BASED ON PSALM 32:5

Be merciful to me, O God,
because of your constant love.
Because of your great mercy
wipe away my sins.

Create a pure heart in me, O God,
and put a new and loyal spirit in me.
Give me again the joy that comes from your salvation,
and make me willing to obey you.

PSALM 51:1, 10, 12

Take my wrongdoing
and throw it away,
down in the deep of the sea;
welcome me into your kingdom of love
for all of eternity.

Based on Micah 7:18–20

Jesus, guide your straying sheep
from the wild mountain steep
to where meadow grass grows deep
and the quiet waters sleep.

Based on Jesus' saying, "I am the good shepherd": John 10:7–16

God, have mercy on me, a sinner!

From Jesus' parable of the Pharisee and the tax collector, Luke 18:13

Trusting in God

The Lord is my shepherd;
I have everything I need.
He lets me rest in fields of green grass
and leads me to quiet pools of fresh water.
He gives me new strength.
He guides me in the right paths,
as he has promised.
Even if I go through the deepest darkness,
I will not be afraid, Lord,
for you are with me.
Your shepherd's rod and staff protect me.

You prepare a banquet for me,
where all my enemies can see me;
you welcome me as an honoured guest
and fill my cup to the brim.
I know that your goodness and love will be with me
   all my life;
and your house will be my home as long as I live.

PSALM 23

The Lord is my light and my salvation;
I will fear no one.
The Lord protects me from all danger;
I will never be afraid.

PSALM 27:1

As Jesus taught

"When you pray," said Jesus to his followers, "do not use a lot of meaningless words… Your Father already knows what you need before you ask him. This, then, is how you should pray:

"Our Father in heaven,
hallowed be your name,
your kingdom come,
your will be done,
on earth as in heaven.
Give us today our daily bread.
Forgive us our sins
as we forgive those who sin against us.
Lead us not into temptation
but deliver us from evil."

THE LORD'S PRAYER

For the kingdom, the power,
and the glory are yours
now and for ever.
Amen.

A TRADITIONAL ENDING FOR THE PRAYER

I will choose the narrow path,
I will walk the straight,
Through the wide and winding world
Up to heaven's gate.

BASED ON MATTHEW 7:13–14

Lord God,
Help me to love you with all my heart, with all my soul,
and with all my mind.
Help me to love other people as much as myself.

BASED ON JESUS' WORDS ABOUT THE COMMANDMENTS, MATTHEW 22:37–40

Dear God,
Help me to love my enemies.
Show me how to do good things for those who hurt me.
Remind me to pray for those who are unkind.

BASED ON LUKE 6:27–28

Lord Jesus,
You told us to love one another.
May I be eager to help others.
May I not think myself more important than them.
May I follow your example of serving others.

BASED ON JESUS' NEW COMMANDMENT IN JOHN 13

FOLLOWING THE WAY

May we help one another
to follow Jesus;

May we encourage one another
to follow Jesus;

May we forgive one another
as Jesus forgives us.

BASED ON PAUL'S LETTER TO ROMAN CHRISTIANS, ROMANS 12

Open my mind, O Lord,
to see your light.

Open my mind, O Lord,
to know the hope to which you have called me.

Open my mind, O Lord,
to see the wonderful blessings you have promised.

Open my mind, O Lord,
to see your power at work in me.

BASED ON PAUL'S LETTER TO THE CHRISTIANS IN EPHESUS,
EPHESIANS 1:18

Spirit of God, put love in my life.
Spirit of God, put joy in my life.
Spirit of God, put peace in my life.
Spirit of God, make me patient.
Spirit of God, make me kind.
Spirit of God, make me good.
Spirit of God, give me faithfulness.
Spirit of God, give me humility.
Spirit of God, give me self-control.

BASED ON PAUL'S LETTER TO THE CHRISTIANS IN GALATIA, GALATIANS 5:22–23

Help me, Lord, to show your love.

Help me to be patient and kind, not jealous or conceited or proud. May I never be ill-mannered, selfish or irritable; may I be quick to forgive and forget.

May I not gloat over wrongdoing, but rather be glad about things that are good and true.

May I never give up loving: may my faith and hope and patience never come to an end.

BASED ON PAUL'S LETTER TO THE CHRISTIANS IN CORINTH, 1 CORINTHIANS 13:4–7

Seeking God's kingdom

Dear God,
I am a child.
Welcome me
into your kingdom.

Based on Matthew 18:1–5

The kingdom of God
is like a tree
growing through all eternity.

In its branches, birds may nest;
in its shade we all may rest.

A prayer inspired by Jesus' parable of the
mustard seed, Matthew 13

May God's peaceable kingdom be
free from every enmity;
wolves and sheep together roam,
goats with leopards make their home,
cows with tiny calves draw near
to bears and lions without fear;
and may a child prepare the way
to heaven's bright eternal day.

Based on Isaiah's foretelling of Jesus,
Isaiah 11:6–9

THE CHRISTIAN LIFE

Day by day,
dear Lord, of thee
three things I pray:
to see thee more clearly,
love thee more dearly,
follow thee more nearly,
day by day.

RICHARD, BISHOP OF CHICHESTER (1197–1253)

Day one: Wisdom

I will live this day thoughtfully so that, if my guardian angel
were to give an account of it, I would not be ashamed.

From the *Resolutions* of St Conrad of Parzham (1818–94)

O Great Spirit, whose voice I hear in the wind,
Whose breath gives life to all the world:
Hear me. I need your strength and wisdom.
Let me walk in beauty.
Open my eyes to see the wonders of the earth and the heavens.
Make my hands respect the things you have made,
and my ears sharp to hear your voice.
Keep my thoughts centred on what is good and lovely.
Give me the strength to help others with gladness and humility.
Make me always ready to come to you
with clean hands and straight eyes.

A prayer from the Navajo tradition

Bless to me, O God,
the work of my hands.
Bless to me, O God,
the work of my mind.
Bless to me, O God,
the work of my heart.

Anonymous

I am only me, but I'm still someone.
I cannot do everything, but I can do something.
Just because I cannot do everything
does not give me the right to do nothing.

Motto from an Amish school in Pennsylvania

May all my deeds
be wheat
not weeds.

Sophie Piper

Day two: Justice

We
not me.

Share
not tear.

Mend
not end

and so
befriend.

SOPHIE PIPER

O God,
Gather together as one
those who believe in peace.
Gather together as one
those who believe in justice.
Gather together as one
those who will stand up
for what it right
and face what comes towards them
with courage and cheerfulness.

Grandfather, Great Spirit:
All over the world the faces of living things are alike.
You have fashioned them with tenderness from the clay.
Look upon your children, that they may face the winds
and walk the good road to the day of quiet.
Grandfather, Great Spirit:
Fill us with the light of your wisdom.
Give us the strength to understand and the eyes to see.
Teach us to walk the soft earth as relatives to all that
    live.

SIOUX PRAYER

We share the earth
we share the sky
we share the shining sea
with those we trust
with those we fear:
we are God's family.

33

Day three: Self-control

Lord and Master of my life,
Save me from laziness, meddling, ambition and gossip.
Make me wise, humble, patient and loving.
May I see my own faults and not judge others.

Lenten prayer of St Ephraim the Syrian

May I be no one's enemy, and may I be the friend of that which
lasts for ever.

May I never quarrel with those nearest: and if I do, may I be quick
to restore the friendship.

May I love only what is good: always seek it and work to achieve it.

May I wish for everyone to find happiness and not envy anyone
their good fortune.

May I never gloat when someone who has wronged me suffers ill
fortune.

When I have done or said something wrong, may I not wait to be
told off, but instead be angry with myself until I have put things
right.

May I win no victory that harms either me or those who compete
against me.

May I help those who have quarrelled to be friends with each other again.

May I, as far as I can, give practical help to my friends and anyone who is in need.

May I never fail a friend who is in danger.

When I visit those who are grieving, may
I find the right words to help heal their pain.

May I respect myself.

May I always control my emotions.

May I train myself to be gentle
and not allow myself to become
angry.

May I never whisper about
wicked people and the things
they have done, but rather
seek to spend my time
with good people and to
follow their example.

EUSEBIUS (3RD CENTURY, ADAPTED)

35

DAY FOUR: ENDURANCE

Teach us, Lord,
to serve you as you deserve,
to give and not to count the cost,
to fight and not to heed the wounds,
to toil and not to seek for rest,
to labour and not to ask for any reward
save that of knowing that we do your will.

St Ignatius Loyola (1491–1556)

Hold on to what is good, even if it is a handful of earth.
Hold on to what you believe in, even if it is a tree that
stands by itself.
Hold on to what you must do, even if it is a long way
from here.
Hold on to life, even when it is easier letting go.
Hold on to love, even when you feel you are all alone.

Pueblo blessing

May I do the best things
in the worst times
and hope them
in the most calamitous.

After a church inscription in praise of Sir Robert Shirley

Day five: Faith

My faith is like a slender tree:
scarce enough to shelter me
from the rain and from the heat;
yet here, alone, with God I meet.

O God,
Help me to believe in you
and to trust in your love and justice.
Let my faith change the way I think and the things I do.
Let it bring me peace and gladness.
Let it prompt me to serve others with humility and kindness.
Let it strengthen me for whatever the day may bring.

Alone with none but thee, my God,
I journey on my way.
What need I fear, when thou art near
O king of night and day?
More safe am I within thy hand
Than if a host did round me stand.

St Columba (521–97)

O gracious and holy Father,
give us wisdom to believe in you,
intelligence to understand you,
diligence to seek you,
patience to wait for you,
eyes to see you,
a heart to meditate upon you,
and a life to declare your greatness to all the world.

Adapted from a prayer attributed to St Benedict (480–543)

DAY SIX: HOPE

My life flows on in endless song;
Above earth's lamentation
I hear the sweet though far-off hymn
That hails a new creation:
Through all the tumult and the strife
I hear the music ringing;
It finds an echo in my soul –
How can I keep from singing?

What though my joys and comforts die?
The Lord my Saviour liveth;
What though the darkness gather round!
Songs in the night he giveth:
No storm can shake my inmost calm
While to that refuge clinging;
Since Christ is Lord of heaven and earth,
How can I keep from singing?

ROBERT LOWRY (1826–99)

May God's will be done by us
Christ's kingdom be begun by us
God's Spirit be surrounding us
And heaven open wide for us.

As long as the moon shall rise,
as long as the stream shall flow,
may the great love from heaven
reach down to the earth below.

As long as the grass shall grow,
as long as the sun shall shine,
may peace surround all the world
and may heaven's joy be mine.

SOPHIE PIPER

All shall be Amen and Alleluia.
We shall rest and we shall see.
We shall see and we shall know.
We shall know and we shall love.
We shall love and we shall praise.

ST AUGUSTINE (354–430)

Day seven: Love

We can do no great things,
Only small things with great love.

Blessed Teresa of Calcutta (1910–97)

Where there is love
God also is there.

Ubi caritas

Love is giving, not taking,
mending, not breaking,
trusting, believing,
never deceiving,
patiently bearing
and faithfully sharing
each joy, every sorrow,
today and tomorrow.

Anonymous

Blessed is the one who truly loves
and does not ask to be loved in return.
Blessed is the one who serves
and does not ask to be served.
Blessed is the one who fears
and does not ask to be feared.
Blessed is the one who does good to others
and does not ask that others do good in return.

BASED ON WORDS BY BROTHER GILES (DIED 1251)

Lord, make me an instrument of your peace.
Where there is hatred, let me sow love;
Where there is injury, pardon;
Where there is discord, union;
Where there is doubt, faith;
Where there is despair, hope;
Where there is darkness, light;
Where there is sadness, joy.

O divine Master, grant that I may not so much seek
to be consoled as to console, to be understood as
to understand, to be loved as to love; for it is in
giving that we receive, it is in pardoning that we
are pardoned, and it is in dying that we are born to
eternal life.

ATTRIBUTED TO ST FRANCIS OF ASSISI (1181–1226)

PLANET EARTH

Here on the ancient rock of earth
I sit and watch the sky;
I feel the breeze that moves the trees
While stately clouds float by.
I wonder why our planet home
Spins round and round the sun
And what will last for ever
When earth's days all are done.

AROUND THE YEAR

All that we see rejoices in the sunshine,
All that we hear makes merry in the Spring:
God grant us such a mind to be glad after our kind,
And to sing
His praises evermore for everything.

Christina Rossetti (1830–94)

We plough the land,
God sends the rain
to bring the harvest
once again;
and when the fields
of wheat turn gold,
then God's great goodness
must be told.

Based on Psalm 65

This simply lovely day –
      I want to share it.
There is no beauty with which
      to compare it.
Each green, each blue,
      each changing hue –
I hardly understand
      how heav'n can spare it.

Now the wind is coming,
Now the wind is strong,
Now the winter freezes
And the darkness will be long.
Now we see the starlight
In the midnight sky,
We know God is with us
And the angels are close by.

CREATURES GREAT AND SMALL

I think of the diverse majesty
of all the creatures on earth –
some with the power to terrify
and others that only bring mirth.
I think of their shapes and their colours,
their secret and curious ways,
and my heart seems to long for a language
to sing their Great Maker's praise.

All things bright and beautiful,
All creatures great and small,
All things wise and wonderful,
The Lord God made them all.

CECIL FRANCES ALEXANDER (1818–95)

He prayeth best, who loveth best
All things both great and small;
For the dear God who loveth us,
He made and loveth all.

SAMUEL TAYLOR COLERIDGE (1772–1834)

Multicoloured animals
With stripes and dots and patches:
God made each one different –
There isn't one that matches.

49

THE BIRDS OF THE AIR

God bless the birds of springtime
that twitter in the trees
and flutter in the hedgerows
and soar upon the breeze.

God bless the birds of summer
that gather on the shore
and glide above the ocean
where breakers crash and roar.

God bless the birds of autumn
as they prepare to fly
and fill the damp and chilly air
with wild and haunting cry.

God bless the birds of winter
that hop across the snow
and peck the fallen seeds and fruits
of summer long ago.

Listen, all you birds of the air:
You should learn to praise your Maker,
who has given you the freedom of the skies,
who provides you with food that grows wild and free
and clear water in the tumbling streams;
who has made for you homes in the mountain crags
and the marshy valleys according to your kind;
who has told the trees to grow tall and strong,
so you can build your nests in safety;
who clothes you and your young in soft down and
  bright feathers.
Seeing that God has blessed you so much,
you should beware of ingratitude
and learn to sing your songs of praise.

ADAPTED FROM THE WORDS OF ST FRANCIS OF ASISSI (1181–1226)

The wild birds are calling out
their wild morning song
to praise the Maker God
to whom wild things belong.

GREEN AND GROWING THINGS

Who would make a tiny flower
so beautiful? It lasts an hour!
The bloom then quickly fades away
before the setting of the day.

Who would make a tiny leaf
so intricate? Its life is brief:
a season in the summer sun
before its fluttering life is done.

The One who made both great and small,
who loves and cares for one and all
on land and water, sky and sea:
the One who loves and cares for me.

Thank you, great maker God, for plants that
live in dangerous places, clinging to cliffs and
crags and crumbling walls. Thank you for their
unexpected beauty.

Where the earth is ripped and torn
weave a web of green,
and add a patch of flowers so
the mend cannot be seen.

The trees grow down,
down into the earth,
right down into long ago.

The trees grow up,
up into the sky
right up where the strong winds blow.

The trees, they sway,
they sway in the wind
and whisper a secret song:

"We thank you, God,
for keeping us safe,
that we might grow tall and strong."

LITTLE THINGS

The little bugs that scurry,
The little beasts that creep
Among the grasses and the weeds
And where the leaves are deep:
All of them were made by God
As part of God's design.
Remember that the world is theirs,
Not only yours and mine.

Create a space for little things:
Bejewelled bugs with buzzing wings
And pudgy grubs that bravely cling
To slender stems that bend and swing.

Create a calm for quiet things:
For timid birds too shy to sing
And breaths of wind that softly linger
In the blossom trees of spring.

CHRISTINA GOODINGS

Dear Father, hear and bless
your beasts and singing birds;
and guard with tenderness
small things that have no words.

EDITH RUTTER LEATHAM (1870–1939)

We give thanks for domestic animals.
Those creatures who can trust us enough
to come close. Those creatures who can
trust us enough to be true to themselves.

They approach us from the wild. They
approach us from the inner world. They
bring beauty and joy, comfort and peace.
For this miracle and for the lesson of this
miracle, we give thanks.

Amen.

MICHAEL LEUNIG

When little creatures die
And it's time to say goodbye
To a bright-eyed furry friend,
We know that God above
Will remember them with love:
A love that will never end.

Respect the earth

O God,
You set the patterns of the world –
summer and winter,
seedtime and harvest –
so that all living things may flourish.

But we have been greedy
for warmth in wintertime
cool air in summertime
harvest crops at seedtime
spring flowers as the year grows old.

Teach us to live peaceably with the world.
Let the patterns be restored
and bless us.

Sophie Piper

May planet earth
go round and round
yet may our dreams
be heaven bound.

Our world is broken
and we must mend it.

It is our home;
we dare not end it.

The earth lies bare
so we shall tend it.

We pray for help:
and God will send it.

Sophie Piper

Save me a clean stream, flowing
to unpolluted seas;

lend me the bare earth, growing
untamed flowers and trees.

May I share safe skies
when I wake, every day,

with birds and butterflies?
Grant me a space where I can play

with water, rocks, trees, and sand;
lend me forests, rivers, hills, and sea.

Keep me a place in this old land,
somewhere to grow, somewhere to be.

Jane Whittle

A WORLDWIDE FAMILY

May we learn to appreciate different points of view:

to know that the view from the hill is different from the view
  in the valley;
the view to the east is different from the view to the west;
the view in the morning is different from the view in the evening;
the view of a parent is different from the view of a child;
the view of a friend is different from the view of a stranger;
the view of humankind is different from the view of God.

May we all learn to see what is good, what is true, what is
worthwhile.

Home and family

Dear God, bless all my family,
as I tell you each name;
and please bless each one differently
for no one's quite the same.

Bless all our families, dear God.
May they be a place of kindness and forgiveness, where
everyone can learn to be truly themselves.

In all the times we've loved and laughed
And fought and rowed and hated
We give a cautious thanks for those
To whom we are related.

Dear Lord,
Please let our house be a home full of love –
a welcoming place for our family and friends. May it be
cosy and warm and light – and brimming with laughter
and joy.

JENNI DUTTON

Thank you, dear God, for the little place that is my
home – more special to me than all the stars in the
universe.

My home is not a roof above
my home is not a floor
my home is not a window
and my home is not a door.

My home is where I laugh aloud
my home is where I weep
my home is where I lay me down
all safe and sound to sleep.

My home is in the sheltering
of angels from above
and in the faith and hope I have
in God's unfailing love.

TABLE GRACES

For health and strength
and daily food,
we praise your name,
O Lord.

TRADITIONAL

Let us take a moment
To thank God for our food,
For friends around the table
And everything that's good.

Dear God,
I gratefully bow my head
To thank you for my daily bread,
And may there be a goodly share
On every table everywhere. Amen.

MENNONITE CHILDREN'S PRAYER

The bread is warm and fresh,
The water cool and clear.
Lord of all life, be with us,
Lord of all life, be near.

AFRICAN GRACE

The harvests have ripened in the sun;
There's plenty of food for everyone:
There's some for ourselves and more to share
With all of God's people everywhere.

The Lord is good to me,
And so I thank the Lord
For giving me the things I need,
The sun, the rain, the appleseed.
The Lord is good to me.

Attributed to John Chapman, planter of orchards (1774–1845)

Harvest of leaf,
Harvest of fruit,
Harvest of stem,
Harvest of root;
Harvest of lowland,
Harvest of hill,
Harvest that all
May eat their fill.

Friends around us

O God,
We give thanks for the goodhearted people who love us and do good to us and who show their mercy and kindness by providing us with food and drink, house and shelter when we are in trouble or in need.

FROM A 1739 PRAYER BOOK

Thank you, dear God, for the many people who help us when we are out and about:

those who are extra helpful in making sure we find our way;
those who are extra watchful to make sure we stay out of danger;
those who are extra kind in making sure we get home safely.

Thank you, dear God, for the many strangers who are not a danger, but a blessing.

Believe in yourself and think well of others;
Believe in others and show them your love;
Believe in the love that exceeds human knowing:
Within and beyond, below and above.

Dear God,
Help me to make good friends
who make it easy for me to be a good person.
Help me to walk away from bad friends
who make it easy for me to be a bad person.

Dear God,

May we sit down with friends through all our days:

On the plastic chairs of playgroup,

On the wooden chairs at school,

On the soft and sagging sofas of home,

On the folding chairs of holidays,

On the fashionable seats of restaurants

And on the dusty seats in the garden

Till at last, when we have grown old,

We need our friends to help us in and out of chairs.

For a better world

O God, help us not to despise or oppose what we do not understand.

William Penn (1644–1718)

I am a city pilgrim:
with God I walk the street,
looking for the face of Christ
in everyone I meet.

May all the people of the world have a place where they can make their home.
May they live without quarrel.
May they live without enmity.
May they live in freedom and prosper.

O God,
Settle the quarrels among the nations.

May they hammer their swords into ploughs and their spears into pruning knives…

Where the tanks now roll, let there be tractors;
where the landmines explode, let the fields grow crops.

Let there be a harvest of fruit and grain
and peace that the world can share.

Based on Micah 4:3–5

Lord, watch over refugees,
their tired feet aching.
Help them bear their heavy loads,
their backs breaking.
May they find a place of rest,
no fears awake them.
May you always be their guide,
never forsake them.

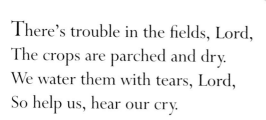

There's trouble in the fields, Lord,
The crops are parched and dry.
We water them with tears, Lord,
So help us, hear our cry.

There's trouble in our hearts, Lord,
The world is full of pain.
Set us to work for healing,
Send blessings down like rain.

Dear God,
When everything is going wrong I sometimes wonder why you let
bad things happen.

But then you open my eyes to the majesty of your world, and
I know once more that you are far greater than I can imagine,
and I believe once more that your love and goodness will not be
overcome.

BASED ON THE BOOK OF JOB

PEACE

Peace for the seed
and peace for the flower,
peace for each sunlit
golden hour.

Peace for the garden,
peace for the field,
peace for the harvests'
golden yield.

Peace for a season,
peace for a year,
peace for a lifetime –
world without fear.

SOPHIE PIPER

The olive tree I thought was dead
has opened new green leaves instead
and where the fighting scarred the earth
now poppies dance with joy and mirth.

The doves build nests, they coo and sigh
beside the fields where corn grows high
and grapes hang heavy on the vine,
and those who fought share bread and wine.

FESTIVALS

Harvest time is gold and red:
Thank you, God, for daily bread.
Christmas time is red and green:
Heaven now on earth is seen.
Easter time is green and white:
Bring us all to heaven's light.
Pentecost is white and gold:
God's own spirit makes us bold.

Harvest

Thank you, dear God, for our harvest garden.
Thank you for the seeds and the soil,
for the sun and the rain,
for the roots and the leaves and the ripening fruits.
As you have blessed us with harvest gifts, dear God,
may we bless others by sharing them.

Lord, help those who plant and sow,
weed and water, rake and hoe,
toiling in the summer heat
for the food they need to eat.

Bless the work of their tired hands:
turn their dry and dusty lands
to a garden, green and gold,
as their harvest crops unfold.

Thank you for the orchard,
thank you for the field,
thank you for the garden
and the harvest yield.

Thank you for the wild wood
where nuts and berries fall
and for the wild harvest
for wild creatures all.

We plough the fields, and scatter
The good seed on the land.
But it is fed and watered by God's almighty hand.
He sends the snow in winter,
The warmth to swell the grain,
The breezes and the sunshine,
And soft refreshing rain:
All good gifts around us are sent from heaven above;
Then thank the Lord, O thank the Lord,
For all his love.

MATTHIAS CLAUDIUS (1740–1815)

CHRISTMAS

Let us travel to Christmas
By the light of a star.
Let us go to the hillside
Right where the shepherds are.
Let us see shining angels
Singing from heaven above.
Let us see Mary cradling
God's holy child with love.

The wise men read the skies above,
and now we read their story
of how they found the prince of peace,
newborn from heaven's glory.

We come, as if to Bethlehem,
to offer gifts of love
to make this world at Christmas time
a piece of heaven above.

Christmas is about a birth:
a child from heaven and peace on earth.

Christmas is about a night
transformed by heaven's shining light.

Christmas is about God's love
that reaches down from heaven above.

God, our loving Father, help us remember the birth of Jesus,
that we may share in the song of the angels, the gladness of the
shepherds and the wisdom of the wise men.

May the Christmas morning make us happy to be your children and
the Christmas evening bring us to our beds with grateful thoughts,
forgiving and forgiven, for Jesus' sake.

Amen.

ROBERT LOUIS STEVENSON (1850–94)

Rejoice and be merry
in songs and in mirth!
O praise our Redeemer,
all mortals on earth!
For this is the birthday
of Jesus our King,
Who brought us salvation –
his praises we'll sing!

ANONYMOUS

EASTER

Come, Holy Angels,
into this dark night.
Roll away the stone of death.
Let the light of life
shine from heaven.

Lord Jesus, who died upon the cross:
You know this world's suffering,
You know this world's sorrowing,
You know this world's dying.

Lord Jesus, who rose again, in your name
I will work for this world's healing,
I will work for this world's rejoicing,
I will work for this world's living.

The autumn leaves were laid to rest
But now the trees are green,
And signs that God brings all to life
Throughout the world are seen.

And Jesus is alive, they say,
And death is not the end.
We rise again in heaven's light
With Jesus as our friend.

ASCENSION AND PENTECOST

Let the Spirit come
like the winds that blow:
take away my doubts;
help my faith to grow.

Let the Spirit come
like a flame of gold:
warm my soul within;
make me strong and bold.

Dear God,
We think of the people
we know today
who help us
to follow Jesus.

We think of the people
from days gone by
whose stories help us
to follow Jesus.

We think of their wise words
and their good deeds
and ask you to help us
to follow Jesus.

Lord Jesus,
I have chosen to follow you
in the path of righteousness
and I will not look back.

May I serve you
by feeding the hungry.

May I serve you
by clothing those in need.

May I serve you
by caring for the oppressed.

May I recognize you
in everyone I serve.

A PRAYER INSPIRED BY THE WORDS OF JESUS, MATTHEW 25:31–46

Christ has no body now on earth but yours,
no hands but yours, no feet but yours…
Yours are the feet with which he is to go about doing good,
and yours are the hands with which he is to bless us now.

ST TERESA OF AVILA (1515–82)

IN TIMES OF NEED

As the rain hides the stars,
as the autumn mist hides the hills,
as the clouds veil the blue of the sky,
so the dark happenings of my lot
hide the shining of your face from me.
Yet, if I may hold your hand in the darkness,
it is enough.
Since I know that, though I may stumble in my going,
you do not fall.

GAELIC PRAYER (TRANSLATED BY ALISTAIR MACLEAN)

Sickness and health

Dear God,
I pray for someone who is unwell.
Soothe their pain,
calm their worries,
bless them with sleep,
bring them your healing.

Dear God, let me sleep the aching away.
Dear God, let me sleep the weakness away.
Dear God, let me sleep the tiredness away.
Dear God, let me sleep the long hours away.

O God,
Please heal me.
Make me stronger in body
and merrier in mind.

Some people serve God with their strength.
Some people serve God with their weakness.
Some people serve God with their cleverness.
Some people serve God with their simplicity.
May I serve you, Lord God, as myself.

Dear God,
Let me hear the laughter of angels.

Bless my teeth, O Lord, I pray,
For I brush them night and day;
Keep them safe, Lord, I implore,
In my mouth for evermore.

Yesterday was difficult.
Today was hard.
Tomorrow will be tough.
In times of trouble,
keep close to me, God,
and remind me of your everlasting comfort
for those in need.

Victoria Tebbs

PARTINGS

We stand at a parting of the ways.
We thank God for the companionship we have enjoyed,
for the things we have done together
and the things we have learned together.

We ask God to bless us as we go our separate ways,
knowing there will be uphills and downhills,
good times and bad times.

We pray that we will find new friendships and new challenges.
We pray that God will give us faith and hope at all times,
and surround us with unfailing love.

May the road rise to meet you.
May the wind be always at your back.
May the sun shine warm upon your face,
the rains fall soft upon your fields and,
until we meet again,
may God hold you in the palm of his hand.

Irish blessing

Darkest hours

Danger and trial
God's love cannot sever;
it binds me to life
here and now and for ever.

O God,
Lift me when I fall;
forgive me when I fail.

Flood of sorrow, flood of tears
Like the flood of ancient years

Now in grief my world is drowned
Storm and cloud are all around

Pull me to the ark of love
Set your rainbow high above

Let my world grow new and green
Let the tree of peace be seen.

O God,
Put an end to death.
Put an end to grief and crying and pain.
Make all things new.
Lead us to heaven.

From Revelation 21

Every day
in silence we remember

those whom we loved
to whom we have said a last goodbye.

Every day
in silence we remember.

O God, our help in ages past,
our hope for years to come,
be thou our guard while troubles last,
and our eternal home.

Isaac Watts (1674–1748)

BLESSINGS

May the Lord bless you,
may the Lord take care of you;
May the Lord be kind to you,
may the Lord be gracious to you;
May the Lord look on you with favour,
may the Lord give you peace.

FROM NUMBERS 6:24–26

NIGHT PRAYERS

Now I lay me down to sleep,
I pray thee, Lord, thy child to keep;
Thy love to guard me through the night
And wake me in the morning light.

TRADITIONAL

Lord, keep us safe this night,
Secure from all our fears;
May angels guard us while we sleep,
Till morning light appears.

JOHN LELAND (1754–1841)

Angels surround me
Each hour, every place,
Leading my soul
To the high king of grace.

Angel of God, my guardian dear
To whom God's love commits me here,
Ever this day be at my side
To light and guard, to rule and guide.

TRADITIONAL

GOD BLESS US EVERY ONE

May God's blessing come from far
Shining like the morning star
Showing clear my path to me
Guiding to eternity.

God bless all those that I love,
God bless all those that love me;
God bless all those that love those that I love
And all those that love those that love me.

FROM AN OLD SAMPLER

For blessings here
and those in store
we give thanks now
and evermore.

Trust in the Lord
and do good
so you may dwell
in safety.

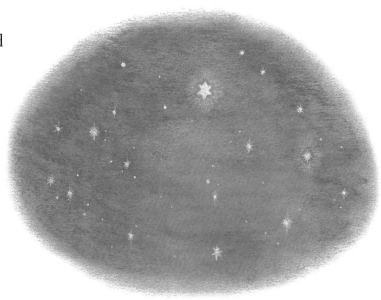

May neighbours respect you,
trouble neglect you,
the angels protect you
and heaven accept you.

IRISH BLESSING

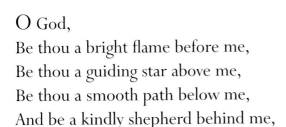

O God,
Be thou a bright flame before me,
Be thou a guiding star above me,
Be thou a smooth path below me,
And be a kindly shepherd behind me,
Today, tonight, and for ever.

FROM CARMINA GADELICA

Deep peace of the running waves to you,
Deep peace of the flowing air to you,
Deep peace of the quiet earth to you,
Deep peace of the shining stars to you,
Deep peace of the shades of night to you,
Moon and stars always giving light to you,
Deep peace of Christ, the Son of Peace, to you.

TRADITIONAL GAELIC BLESSING

INDEX OF FIRST LINES